TIME
FOR KIDS

Survival!
OCEAN

William B. Rice

Consultants

Timothy Rasinski, Ph.D.
Kent State University

Lori Oczkus
Literacy Consultant

Based on writing from
TIME For Kids. TIME For Kids and the *TIME For Kids* logo are registered trademarks of TIME Inc. Used under license.

Publishing Credits

Dona Herweck Rice, *Editor-in-Chief*
Lee Aucoin, *Creative Director*
Jamey Acosta, *Senior Editor*
Heidi Fiedler, *Editor*
Lexa Hoang, *Designer*
Stephanie Reid, *Photo Editor*
Rane Anderson, *Contributing Author*
Rachelle Cracchiolo, *M.S.Ed., Publisher*

Image Credits: p.33 (top) BigStock; p.35 (spear) Corbis; p.25 (top) Dreamstime; pp.4–5, 11 (top), pp.12–13, 19 (fingers), pp.26–27, 35 (top), p.37 (bottom), p.38 (background) Getty Images; pp.8–9, 16, 28, 31, 41 Timothy J. Bradley; p.26 (bottom) NASA; pp.14–15 Kristof, Emory/National Geographic Stock; p.20; Photo Researchers, Inc.; pp.6–7 Allpix/Splash News/Newscom; p.7 (top) Imago Stock/Newscom; p.37 (top) Marlene Karas/Newscom; p.39 The Granger Collection, New York; p.48 William Rice; All other images from Shutterstock.

Teacher Created Materials

5301 Oceanus Drive
Huntington Beach, CA 92649-1030
http://www.tcmpub.com
ISBN 978-1-4333-4819-8
© 2013 Teacher Created Materials, Inc.

TABLE OF CONTENTS

Lost at Sea! 4

Safety First! 10

Exposed! 18

Thirsty! 23

SOS 26

Hungry! 32

I Will Survive! 36

Glossary 42

Index 44

Bibliography 46

More to Explore 47

About the Author 48

LOST AT SEA!

"Help! Help!" you scream into the salty air. But the rushing wind drowns out your cries. "Help!" you call again. You hope against hope that someone—anyone—can hear you across the water.

But there is no one. You are alone. You are a **castaway**, adrift and lost at sea. How did this happen? How did you get here? And what can you do to survive?

It seems strange to think of someone lost at sea. Modern boats and technology make it seem impossible. But it does happen. Whenever people are at sea, they should be prepared for anything—even a fight to survive.

THINK LINK

- Find out how to survive a shipwreck.
- Discover how to find food and water when you're lost at sea.
- Learn how to signal for help.

How does someone wind up lost at sea? Most likely, it happens when you're on a cruise ship or fishing boat that crashes or breaks down. Don't worry! Boats usually have the tools you need to survive. So, if you suddenly find yourself in the middle of a disaster, the most important thing you can do is keep your **wits** about you. Then, wait for help to come.

Imagine the unthinkable happens. You are trapped on a sinking boat! It's decision time. Think fast! You will need to consider five key areas of survival. **Flotation**, warmth, freshwater, a signal, and food are all essential. But there is one thing even more important than any of these. It is you. How you act and react is crucial. Thinking clearly and staying calm are the best things you can do to ensure your safety and survival.

X Factors

There are four key factors that affect surviving a shipwreck. They are out of your control, but you can overcome them if you stay calm and think clearly.

location of the wreck

climate

temperature of the water

distance from land

Plane Crash!

It's less likely than a shipwreck, but an airplane can crash into the water. Surviving such a crash is rare, but it is possible. A person in that situation should stay calm and try to grab what is needed to survive.

In the past 400 years, there have been more than 100,000 shipwrecks.

DIG DEEPER!

Anatomy of a Shipwreck

There are many reasons ships sink. Sometimes, a ship crashes into rocks, ice, reefs, or other objects. If a hole forms in the **hull** or body, water floods into the ship. If too much water flows inside, it will begin to sink. Other times, ships carry too much weight and tip over during a storm. Can you find the five key things below that will help someone survive this wreck?

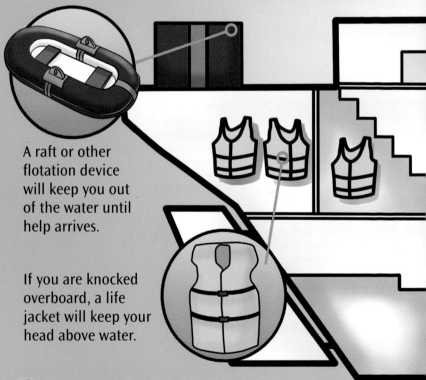

A raft or other flotation device will keep you out of the water until help arrives.

If you are knocked overboard, a life jacket will keep your head above water.

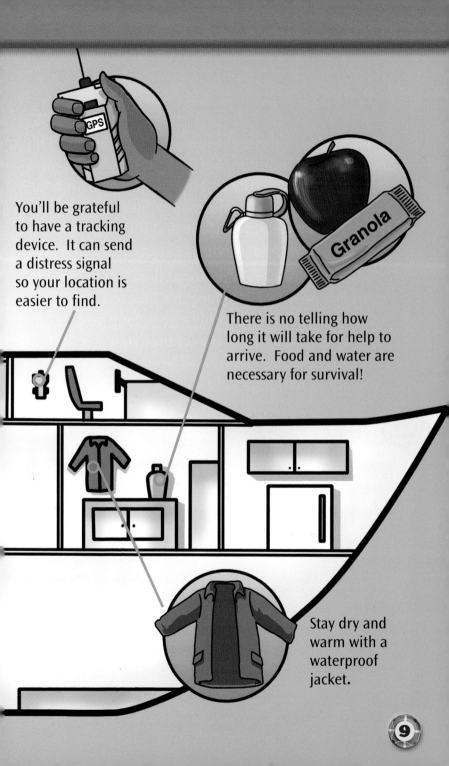

You'll be grateful to have a tracking device. It can send a distress signal so your location is easier to find.

There is no telling how long it will take for help to arrive. Food and water are necessary for survival!

Stay dry and warm with a waterproof jacket.

SAFETY FIRST!

Drowning is the main cause of death at sea. Think about it. How long can you swim or stay afloat on your own? Ten minutes? Thirty minutes? An hour? So, the first order of business is to find a **personal flotation device**. Life jackets and life rings help people float without having to swim or **tread** water.

Boats must have a personal flotation device for everyone on board. If you can't find one, think quickly and find something else to help you stay afloat. Just don't expect that your own strength and ability will keep you afloat for long.

Water Safety on Board a Plane

If you've flown in an airplane, you know about the **inflatable** life vests. There is a second type of flotation device for everyone as well—the seat cushions! They can be strapped on and worn for flotation in a water landing.

Best Case Scenario

Ideally, you'll find an inflatable raft, a **dinghy**, or another **vessel**. A small boat and a life jacket will go far in keeping you safe.

Large cruise ships must keep enough **lifeboats** on board so that every person on the ship has a seat. Fishing boats may store inflatable rafts or small emergency boats. If something happens to the main ship, it is important that all passengers have another option.

Inflatable rafts have proven to be the most seaworthy crafts for surviving storms and heavy seas. They don't **capsize** as easily as regular boats. They are able to move easily in the waves.

It is important that lifeboats are easy to reach and use in an emergency.

Modern Day Pirates

Many people think pirates are a thing of the past. But at this very moment, there are pirates sailing the high seas! Just as in books and movies, modern-day pirates rob, murder, sink ships, and more. The crew on board large ships must always be ready for pirate attacks.

In 2011, the Korean Navy gained control of a ship stolen by Somali pirates.

THE TITANIC

Remember the *Titanic*? It was called the "unsinkable ship." It set sail for the first time on April 10, 1912. It sank five days later after striking an iceberg. The crew wasn't ready for a disaster. There were more than 2,000 passengers on board the ship, but only 20 lifeboats. Over 1,000 people were stranded without lifeboats. They drowned in the freezing water. Even people wearing life jackets died.

The Final Death Toll

No one knows exactly how many people were on board the *Titanic* or how many died. The ship records are not clear. What we do know is that of the nearly 2,200 people on board, more than 1,500 died.

an underwater view of the rusted railing on the *Titanic*

Most of the deaths from the *Titanic* were caused by the water's nearly freezing temperatures.

Unforgettable Shipwrecks

The sinking of the *Titanic* was the most famous shipwreck in history. But it wasn't the worst.

RMS Empress of Ireland

Shipwreck: May 28, 1914

Death Toll: 1,012

On a foggy morning, a Norwegian cargo ship crashed into the *Empress of Ireland*. The cargo ship did not sink. But the *Empress of Ireland* capsized and sank in only 14 minutes.

Sultana

Shipwreck: April 27, 1865

Death Toll: 1,800

A steamboat headed down the Mississippi River was sunk by an explosion on board. Many of the passengers were soldiers who had fought in the Civil War.

MV Le Joola

Shipwreck: September 26, 2002

Death Toll: 1,863

This ferry was only supposed to carry about 580 passengers. But when it sank, it had over 2,000! It only took five minutes for this cargo ship to capsize off the coast of Africa. There was only enough time to load one lifeboat.

Mont-Blanc

Shipwreck: December 6, 1917

Death Toll: 1,950

A great explosion took place when two cargo ships collided in a harbor in Canada. People died on board the ship. Over 9,000 people on shore were injured. The explosion caused a huge **tsunami** that snapped trees and destroyed buildings.

MV Doña Paz

Shipwreck: December 20, 1987

Death Toll: 4,375

A passenger ferry collided with an oil tanker carrying 8,800 barrels of oil. The passenger ferry was only licensed to carry 1,518 passengers. But the crew broke the rules, allowing more than 4,000 to board. Only about 20 passengers survived. Oil filled the waters off the coast of the Philippines.

EXPOSED!

The second leading cause of death on the water is **exposure**. Exposure happens when the body is left unprotected against heat and cold. If the water is cold and you are in it, you can get **hypothermia**. You may even freeze to death. That is one of the reasons it is so important to have a boat or raft to keep you out of the water. You should also have clothing that keeps you warm. Clothing protects a person from the sun, too. All day in the sun on the water can lead to sunburn and **heatstroke**.

Cold Water Survival

It takes energy to survive in cold water. The colder the water, the less time you have—and the faster you need to get help!

Water Temperature (Fahrenheit)	Time Until Death
70°F–80°F	3 hours–unlimited
60°F–70°F	2–40 hours
50°F–60°F	1–6 hours
40°F–50°F	1–3 hours
32.5°F–40°F	30–90 minutes
32.5°F	15–45 minutes

HYPOTHERMIA

Hypothermia occurs when the body's temperature drops a few degrees below normal. If your body gets this cold, you will shiver and become confused. You'll lose control over your muscles. Fingers, toes, and lips will turn blue. As you become numb, you may find your arms and legs don't work. Your pulse and breathing will drop. In time, your organs may stop working. Without immediate help, you can die of hypothermia.

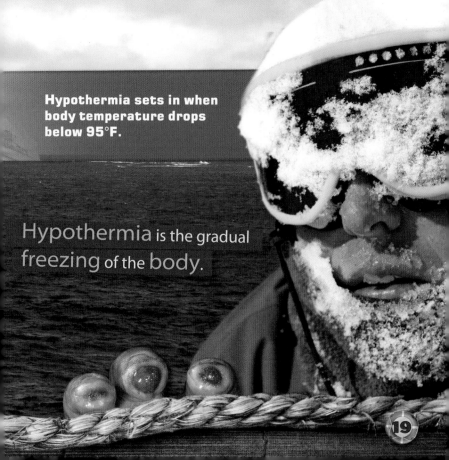

Hypothermia sets in when body temperature drops below 95°F.

Hypothermia is the gradual freezing of the body.

HEATSTROKE

Heatstroke happens when your body temperature rises several degrees above normal. This can happen when the air is very hot. If a person is in the sun, the body may heat up. Normally, you can go indoors to stay cool. At sea, you may not be able to do that. The right clothing will help. Try to wear lightweight, light-colored clothes to stay cool. A hat will also shade the face and head.

Salt Exposure

Saltwater takes away skin's natural moisture. It can dry, chap, and swell the skin. It can also cause rashes and sores over time. It is a good idea to cover up at sea to protect the skin from salt and sun.

If your body starts to heat up, it can mean trouble. Your pulse will speed up. You may have trouble breathing. You may sweat a great deal. This can dry out your body. Your muscles will cramp because they need fluids. When heatstroke occurs, the skin is dry. You may feel dizzy and confused. The body becomes weaker and weaker. Eventually, a person can lose **consciousness**.

In humans, heatstroke occurs when body temperature reaches 105.1°F.

Be Still

Physical activity in high temperatures can cause heatstroke. So it is best to limit activity. Activity uses energy, and a person needs the energy to stay alive.

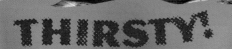

THIRSTY!

Water is one of the most important things a body must have to survive. Our bodies are mostly made of water! You would think that finding water at sea is never a problem. There's water everywhere, right? Well, seawater is saltwater, and that is not what people need to stay healthy. So, what do you do?

You've got to find freshwater. If you have time, grabbing water in a shipwreck is more important than grabbing food. You can live without water for just three to seven days. You can survive much longer without food.

These images show the ratio of salt to water in seawater.

Saltwater or Freshwater?

Normally, people drink freshwater. Water in the ocean is saltwater. Freshwater has only a tiny amount of salt in it, so you can't even taste it. Saltwater is 3 to 5 percent salt. It has a strong salty taste.

60% WATER

The average adult man contains about 10 gallons of water.

You need to be smart about using your water if you have it. You can make a little go a long way. You must **conserve** it. That means you will use just what you need and save the rest for later.

So, what do you do when you run out of water? You have a few options. If it's raining, you're in luck. Water can be collected on a tarp or other plastic material. If you are in a cold area, there may be ice from icebergs. If you are very lucky, you might have a **filter** on your raft. You can use it to filter the salt from seawater and turn it into fresh drinking water.

It is possible to survive for a while on seawater, too. You can drink it. But, over time, the salt will damage your body. If you must drink seawater, don't drink more than about a glass a day.

No Way!

It's strange but true—you can drink your urine if you have to! Urine from a healthy body is mainly water. But it has lots of salt, waste, and other chemicals in it, too. The more you drink, the more those things build up inside you—and over time, that's bad for your health.

A Little at a Time

If the weather is not too hot, water should be carefully rationed. It is possible to survive on less than 32 ounces of water each day.

A man once survived at sea for 62 days on only seawater! He drank very little each day.

If a boat sinks, people usually know about it. They come to help. But finding people at sea is difficult. It's smart to carry a signaling device with you. An **emergency position-indication radio beacon (EPIRB)** is a useful device. It can send a signal to let rescuers know where you are.

The *Swiss Family Robinson* is an adventure novel about a shipwrecked family surviving on a small island in the East Indies.

EPIRB

Got Land?

In some situations, you may be near land. If you can, it's a good idea to try to make your way to shore. But if the **current** is taking you out to sea, you might not want to fight it. Swimming through the waves may use energy you need to survive. One more tip: aim for land with a sandy beach. Rocky beaches or those with cliffs can be dangerous.

EPIRB

Thousands of people are saved by search and rescue teams every year. An EPIRB can save your life! It is an electronic device that tells rescuers you are in trouble, and most ships will have one. You can use it on a ship or while hiking in the mountains. No matter where you are, use the radio beacon to send for help.

1. Use the EPIRB to send a distress call.

5. A rescue team is sent out to find you.

4. A mission control center contacts the authorities.

2. Search and rescue satellites receive the signal.

STOP! THINK...

- Which step do you think is the most important?

- What other steps could you take to help the rescue team find you?

- What would you do if you received a distress call from someone?

3. The signal is sent back to Earth.

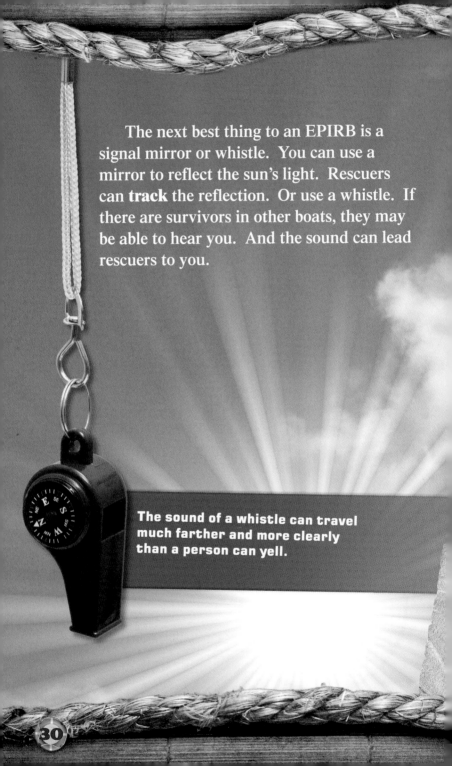

The next best thing to an EPIRB is a signal mirror or whistle. You can use a mirror to reflect the sun's light. Rescuers can **track** the reflection. Or use a whistle. If there are survivors in other boats, they may be able to hear you. And the sound can lead rescuers to you.

The sound of a whistle can travel much farther and more clearly than a person can yell.

How to Signal

Step 1

To signal with a mirror, raise it in front of your face with the reflecting side out. Stretch out your other hand and form a *V* with your thumb and fingers.

Step 2

Move the mirror so you can "capture" the sun's reflection in the *V* of your extended hand.

Step 3

Keep the light in the *V* until the plane is also in the *V*. Now the reflected light will be pointed directly at the plane. Move the mirror slightly to make the signal flash.

Warning: do not do this unless there is an emergency. You should never flash lights at planes for fun.

HUNGRY!

If you're lost at sea, you may get very hungry. Although people need food to live, they can live a long time without it. Even if you have something to eat, you might not have water. It takes a lot of water to **digest** food. It is best to wait to eat until you have collected enough water. You can also survive much longer without food than you can without water.

Most oceans are home to many fish. They are a good source of food. Do some thinking and look at the items you have with you. Can you turn them into a tool to catch fish?

Often, nighttime is the best time to fish. Fish are attracted to bright lights in dark places. If you have a way to make a light, use it to attract the fish.

People in Japan regularly eat raw fish as part of their diets.

A healthy body can survive three to four weeks without food.

If you have a net, you might be able to catch a bird to eat. **Plankton** can also be eaten. You can drag a cloth behind a raft to collect the plankton. Fresh seaweed is also a good source of food. Some of these things may seem unusual. They may not look or smell very good. But remember, we are talking about survival!

Any food high in protein takes a lot of water to digest. Fish, seaweed, and birds have a lot of protein. If you eat too much without drinking water, you will become even more dehydrated. Foods high in carbohydrates are easiest to digest. If you have bread, crackers, rice, or other grains, make your supply last by eating small portions.

seagull

Plankton

Plankton are tiny living things that live in the ocean and drift with the current. They provide food for many sea animals, including whales.

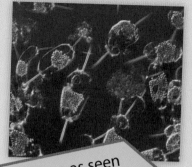

plankton as seen under a microscope

fishing spear

fresh seaweed

I WILL SURVIVE!

With the right tools, you can survive. If you're lost at sea, you may dream of being rescued. Every rescue is amazing. Some are unforgettable!

The Buddy System

A seal helped a Canadian woman survive for eight hours in chilly water. When she fell overboard, she swam for a long time but became exhausted. A seal appeared and stayed by her side until she was rescued! Afterward, she said the seal helped her have a good attitude, which she believes helped her survive.

Dog Adrift

A puppy named Snickers spent 95 days at sea adrift with his owners. The boat finally crashed, and they all swam to a nearby island. However, when a cargo ship rescued his owners, it could not take him aboard. So Snickers spent the next four months surviving alone on the island before he was finally rescued.

76 Days at Sea

Steve Callahan wrote a best-selling book about the days he spent lost at sea. On his journey, he thought the boat he had made was struck by a whale. He survived 76 days in a six-foot life raft. He ate peanuts, cabbages, baked beans, and fish. He had a limited amount of water and caught rainfall when he could.

Saving the Best for Last

Could you survive on a deserted island for a week all by yourself? What about a year? Alexander Selkirk was a Scottish sailor in the early 18th century. He survived for four years on an island off the coast of Chile.

Selkirk had a knife, a musket, gunpowder, carpenter's tools, clothes, a rope, and a Bible with him. He was attacked by rats at night. He had to hunt goats for food. He built huts out of leaves. Over time, his feet became as tough as leather. By the time he was picked up by another vessel, four years had passed! It is said that Selkirk was the inspiration for the classic tale *Robinson Crusoe,* written by Daniel Defoe.

April 30

Having perceived my bread had been low a great while, now I took a survey of it, and reduced myself to one biscuit a day, which made my heart very heavy.

— Robinson Crusoe

Every castaway longs to be rescued.

Alexander Selkirk

Captain's Log

If you are stranded, it is a good idea to pass the time by keeping a record. You should also keep track of the days that pass by. You can make a scratch on the boat every night. Or you can make a calendar by collecting small objects, such as rocks, and grouping them together as the days pass.

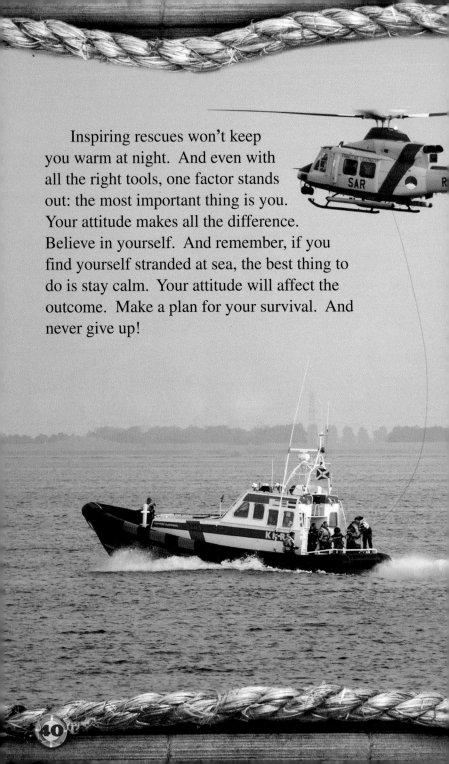

Inspiring rescues won't keep you warm at night. And even with all the right tools, one factor stands out: the most important thing is you. Your attitude makes all the difference. Believe in yourself. And remember, if you find yourself stranded at sea, the best thing to do is stay calm. Your attitude will affect the outcome. Make a plan for your survival. And never give up!

How Would You Survive?

- If you were lost at sea, what would you do first?
- How would you signal for help?
- Would you rather be on a ship or an island by yourself?

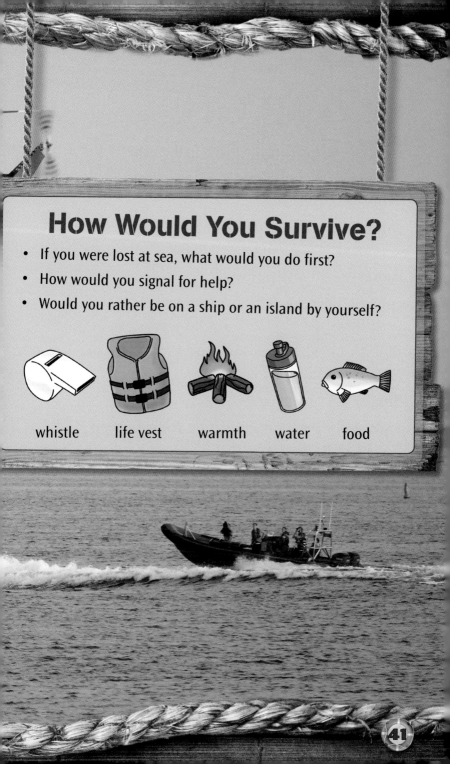

whistle   life vest   warmth   water   food

GLOSSARY

capsize—to turn upside down in the water

castaway—a person who has been shipwrecked and is abandoned or lost

consciousness—the state of being aware of one's thoughts, surroundings, and body

conserve—to save or reserve

current—the flow of water and the speed at which it flows

digest—to break down food inside the body and turn it into nutrition and waste

dinghy—a small boat

emergency position-indication radio beacon (EPIRB)—a device that sends out a signal for rescuers to use to find your location

exposure—the state of being in a bad or harmful situation with nothing to protect you

filter—something that liquid or gas can pass through while solids are trapped

flotation—something that helps floating

heatstroke—an increase in a person's body temperature to a dangerous degree

hull—the bottom of a ship

hypothermia—a dangerous decrease in a person's body temperature

inflatable—able to be filled with air

lifeboats—small boats carried by large boats for use in an emergency

personal flotation device—something that helps the wearer float, for example, a life jacket, a life vest, or a life preserver

plankton—small organisms that live in oceans and provide food for many sea creatures

track—to find someone or something by searching

tread—to keep the head above water and the body straight while staying in one place, usually by moving the arms and legs

tsunami—an unusually large sea wave caused by movements in the earth or volcanic activity

vessel—a craft for traveling on water

wits—mental stability and senses

INDEX

Africa, 17

airplane, 7, 10

Callahan, Stephen, 37

Canada, 17

castaway, 4

Chile, 38

Civil War, 16

clothing, 18, 20

crash, 6–8, 16, 37

cruise ship, 6, 12

current, 27, 35

Defoe, Daniel, 38

dinghy, 11

East Indies, 26

drowning, 10

emergency position indication radio beacon (EPIRB), 26, 28–30

energy, 18, 21, 27

exposure, 18, 20

ferry, 17

filter, 24

fish, 32–34, 37

fishing spear, 35

flotation, 6, 8–10

food, 5–6, 9, 22, 32–35, 38, 41

freshwater, 6, 22–23

heatstroke, 18, 20–21

hypothermia, 18–19

iceberg, 14, 24

island, 26, 37–38, 41

Korean Navy, 13

land, 6, 27

lifeboats, 12, 14

life jacket, 8, 10–11, 14

life vests, 10

mirror, 30–31

Mississippi River, 16

Mont-Blanc, 17

MV Doña Paz, 17

MV Le Joola, 17

personal flotation device, 10

Philippines, 17

pirates, 13

plankton, 34–35

raft, 8, 11–12, 18, 24, 34, 37

RMS Empress of Ireland, 16

Robinson Crusoe, 38

salt, 20, 22–24

saltwater, 20, 22–23

seagull, 34

seal, 36

seaweed, 34–35

Selkirk, Alexander, 38

shipwreck, 5–9, 16–17, 22, 26

signal, 5, 6, 9, 26, 29–31, 41

Snickers, 37

Somali pirates, 13

Sultana, 16

sunburn, 18

Swiss Family Robinson, The, 26

temperature, 6, 15, 18–19, 20–21

Titanic, 14–16

tracking device, 9

tsunami, 17

urine, 24

vessel, 11, 38

warmth, 6, 41

water, 4, 5, 6–10, 12, 14–15, 18, 20, 22–23, 32, 34, 41

waterproof jacket, 9

whistle, 30, 41

BIBLIOGRAPHY

Adams, Simon. *Titanic.* **DK Publishing, 2009.**

See photographs of the underwater wreck of the *Titanic* as you learn all about the history of the ship in this book.

Cerullo, Mary M. *Shipwrecks: Exploring Sunken Cities Beneath the Sea.* **Dutton Children's Books, 2009.**

This book explores the underwater worlds of two different shipwrecks, one a slave ship from the 1700s, and the other a steamship with wealthy passengers on board.

David, Jack. *United States Coast Guard.* **Bellwether Media, 2008.**

The U.S. Coast Guard protects U.S. oceans, waterways, and coastlines. Part of its job is to assist people who become stranded at sea. Learn more about their important work in this book.

Platt, Richard, and Tina Chambers. *Pirate.* **Rev. ed. DK Publishing, 2007.**

Discover pirates across history, from ancient Greece to the 19th century. Information on the different types of ships and vessels is also included.

MORE TO EXPLORE

Diving the Alaskan Frontier
http://www.shipwrecksforkids.com

This website was created by divers to show videos and highlight information about their dives to investigate shipwrecks.

Pirates Info
http://www.piratesinfo.com/

You'll be a pirate expert after learning about the history of pirates, famous pirates, pirate legends, and pirate books.

Online *Titanic* Museum
http://www.onlinetitanicmuseum.com/

This website is a virtual museum that contains a large collection of artifacts related to the *Titanic*. Clear photographs of the artifacts are accompanied by descriptions, making the museum come to life.

National Geographic for Kids
http://kids.nationalgeographic.com/kids/

National Geographic's website for kids provides information on a variety of wildlife and photos and videos of landscapes from around the world, as well as games and other activities.

ABOUT THE AUTHOR

William B. Rice grew up in Pomona, California, and graduated from Idaho State University with a degree in geology. He works at a California state agency that strives to protect the quality of surface and groundwater resources. Protecting and preserving the environment is important to him, and he works to protect oceans and water bodies around the world. He is married with two children and lives in Southern California.